Plant a Pocket of Prairie

Plant a Pocket of Prairie

Phyllis Root

Illustrations by Betsy Bowen

University of Minnesota Press
Minneapolis • London

The University of Minnesota Press
gratefully acknowledges the generous assistance
provided for the publication of this book by the
Margaret W. Harmon Fund.

Published by the University of Minnesota Press
111 Third Avenue South, Suite 290
Minneapolis, MN 55401–2520
http://www.upress.umn.edu

Library of Congress Cataloging-in-Publication Data
Root, Phyllis, author.
Plant a pocket of prairie / Phyllis Root ; illustrations by Betsy Bowen.

ISBN 978-0-8166-7980-5 (hc : alk. paper)
1. Prairie plants—Juvenile literature. I. Bowen, Betsy, illustrator.
II. Title. QK938.P7R66 2014
583'.73—dc23
2013040345

Book design by Brian Donahue / bedesign, inc.
Printed in China on acid-free paper

The University of Minnesota is an equal-opportunity
educator and employer.

20 19 18 17 16 15 14   10 9 8 7 6 5 4 3 2 1

For everyone who works to save
our wild plants and places.
—P.R.

To Carol, Ron, Todd, David G.,
Jeremy, Sheri, Brenda, Gary,
and David O.

Thanks for helping me.
—B.B.

Once prairie stretched
for thousands of miles

an ocean of flowers and grasses,
a sea of sky,
home for bison and elk,
prairie chickens, burrowing owls,
five-lined skinks, Plains garter snakes,
and Ottoe skipper butterflies.

Almost all gone now
to farm and town and city,
even before we knew
all of the things a prairie could do.

But if you want to see
what a prairie might be . . .

Plant a pocket of prairie
in your backyard
or boulevard
or boxes on a balcony.

If you plant a pocket of prairie,
who might come?

Plant foxglove beardtongue.
A ruby-throated hummingbird
might hover and sip and thrum.
If that hummingbird sips and zips
looking for something more to eat . . .

Plant butterfly weed.
Monarch butterflies might lay their eggs
on the undersides of leaves.

And when those monarch eggs hatch
and the larvae turn into hungry butterflies . . .

Plant rough blazing star.
Great spangled fritillaries might show up, too.
If monarchs and fritillaries aren't enough for you . . .

Plant asters.
Silvery checkerspot butterflies might lay their eggs
on the leaves.

Your pocket of prairie might be full
of blooming and buzzing and fluttering.
But don't stop now—

Plant purple coneflowers and Joe Pye weed
and wait for Dakota skippers and swallowtails
to flit and feed.

While you are waiting . . .

Plant goldenrod.
A Great Plains toad
might flick its tongue at goldenrod soldier beetles.

Not enough prairie for you yet?

Plant cup plants.
A thirsty chickadee might come
to drink from a tiny leaf pool.

Plant big bluestem and Indian grass.
Grasshoppers might eat the grass
before grasshopper mice eat the grasshoppers.

More prairie still?

Plant sunflowers,
and goldfinches might dine upside down.

Plant bottle gentian.
A bumblebee might battle inside,
leaving only its bumblebee bottom sticking out.

If your pocket of prairie grows big enough . . .

Plant prairie milkweed and hairy mountain mint,
and breathe sweet air.

A dickcissel might build a nest
and lay four pale blue eggs.
A prairie skink
might guard her eggs beneath a rock.

A meadowlark might fly,
calling *chee-che-chee-chee-chirr*.

If your pocket of prairie grows bigger still
who else might come?
Who knows?

If you plant a pocket of prairie,
and I plant a pocket of prairie,
and everyone we know plants
a pocket of prairie,
and everyone they know plants
a pocket of prairie,
one day we might look out and see

the prairie coming home.

Prairie, Prairie, Everywhere

Once native prairies covered almost forty percent of the United States—wet prairie, black soil prairie, sand prairie, goat prairie, gravel prairie. These prairies were home to hundreds of kinds of plants and animals. When settlers arrived, they plowed the rich prairie soil to plant crops. When prairie was too rocky or rugged to farm, cattle and sheep ate the grass. Less than one percent of that native prairie remains, making prairie one of the most endangered ecosystems in the world.

We can't bring back the prairie as it once was. The great seas of grass, sometimes taller than a person on horseback, with their web of soil, plants, and animals, are gone, along with the enormous herds of bison that lived on the prairie.

Although we cannot bring back the original prairie, we can plant pockets of prairie. Even a little prairie still benefits the insects, birds, and other animals who are at home on the prairie and also preserves the beauty of prairie flowers and grasses.

Prairie plants provide food and homes for butterflies, bees, dragonflies, and a host of other insects, as well as for the birds that eat the insects, the animals that nest in the grasses, and all sorts of prairie life. Especially important, native plants are food for native insects in the larval stage—some plants feed the larvae of hundreds of different native insects. Without milkweed for monarch larvae to eat, for example, there would be no monarch butterflies. Why do native insects matter? Without them, many of our native birds have no source of food. No plants, no insects, no birds—everything is connected. Every native prairie plant helps maintain the ecosystem.

Who knows? Someday my backyard and your backyard and all the other backyards might make a new kind of prairie, a pocket-work prairie, where wildlife can thrive. You might not look out your window and see a bison, but you might see monarchs and warblers and spade foot toads. You will certainly see prairie grasses and flowers like the ones that used to grow as far as the eye could see, to the edge of the sky and beyond.

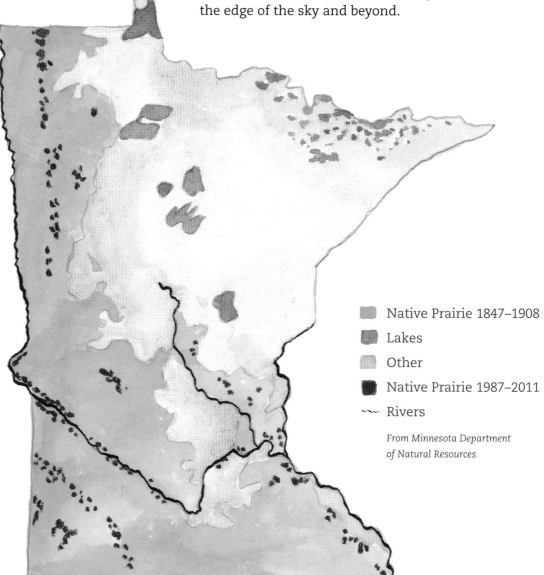

Native Prairie 1847–1908
Lakes
Other
Native Prairie 1987–2011
Rivers

From Minnesota Department of Natural Resources

How to Plant a Pocket of Prairie

Be a prairie detective.

Do research at the library or online and find out what kind of prairie might have grown in your area. Remember that different plants need different amounts of sunlight and water and space. Read in books or online or talk to people who know prairies to see what might grow best in your own pocket of prairie.

Prairies have been called "upside down forests" because of the deep roots of many prairie plants. In a prairie there is more biomass (total amount of living material) under the ground than above ground. The deep roots of prairie plants help them survive drought and wind. Deep-rooted plants don't do well in boxes or pots, but some plants, such as bergamot, black-eyed Susan, large-flowered beardtongue, purple coneflower, purple prairie clover, rattlesnake master, rough blazing star, and spiderwort have shallower root systems and grow well in containers. Others, like big bluestem and compass plant, need to be planted in the earth so their roots can grow many feet deep.

Buy prairie plants or seeds from a reputable nursery that grows its own prairie plants. *Never, ever dig up plants in the wild*. The more kinds of plants in your prairie pocket, the more opportunities you are giving insects, birds, and other animals to find food and shelter.

Be a prairie observer. Every week your pocket of prairie will change. Keep notes of what you plant, how it grows, when it blooms. Watch what comes to your pocket of prairie and write it down. If you don't recognize your visitors, find a guidebook or search online. A world of prairie life comes together when you plant a pocket of prairie seeds.

Animals and Plants

Prairies are rich in numerous flowers and grasses, many with wonderful names. Hundreds of kinds of animals, too, live in prairies, including many insects that survive only on native plants. Here are a few prairie dwellers.

Mammals

Bison *Bison bison*

Up to sixty million bison once grazed the prairie grasses and were food for swift foxes, prairie wolves, eagles, and other animals. Almost all the bison were slaughtered in the 1800s, changing the life of the prairie forever.

Elk *Cervus elaphus*

Herds of elk grazed the prairies before farming plowed the land. Hunters killed most of the elk, and by 1900 almost all the elk had disappeared from the prairie. Elk have been reintroduced in Minnesota, but this is still a species of special concern.

Northern grasshopper mouse

Onychomys leucogaster

Active at night, this mouse plugs its underground tunnels each morning to keep in moisture and keep out dangers. These mice eat grasshoppers, of course, and also other insects, plants, seeds, and even smaller mice.

Birds

Black-capped chickadee *Poecile atricapillus*

These birds love sunflower seeds and can be seen in the fall clinging
to the seed heads at the tops of the plants, eating the seeds.

Burrowing owl *Athene cunicularia*

These small owls live in holes in the ground, either in empty badger or squirrel
burrows or in holes they dig themselves. If they are frightened, they may make a
noise like a rattlesnake. In Minnesota they are listed as endangered.

Dickcissel *Spiza americana*

Dickcissels migrate north to lay their eggs and raise their young. They
build nests on the ground, hidden in grasses. Some people think their
chit chit chee chee call sounds like saying their name: *dick dick cissel*.

American goldfinch *Spinus tristis*

These bright yellow birds eat insects and seeds, which are found
in abundance in a prairie. Goldfinches dip up and down when
they fly. They are sometimes called Wild Canary.

Ruby-throated hummingbird *Archilochus colubris*

The tiniest birds, hummingbirds sip nectar from tube-shaped flowers,
such as foxglove beardtongue, bergamot, butterfly weed, wood lilies,
and Michigan lilies—all of which grow in prairies.

Eastern meadowlark *Sturnella magna*

This bird (not really a lark) has a beautiful call and builds its
nest on the ground. The horned lark (*Eremophila alpestris*), North
America's only native lark, can also be seen in prairies.

Greater prairie chicken *Tympanuchus cupido*

In the spring prairie chickens gather on "booming grounds," open areas
where the males strut and stamp and make a hollow booming call to attract
females; the males leap in the air and inflate orange air sacs in their throats.
In Minnesota prairie chickens are a species of special concern.

Reptiles and Amphibians

Common five-lined skink

Plestiodon fasciatus

Five-lined skinks need prairies and forests with south-facing rock outcrops so they can bask in the sun and stay warm. They are a species of special concern in Minnesota.

Prairie skink

Plestiodon septentrionalis

Skinks are able to break off their tails if grabbed or if threatened. The tail wiggles for a few minutes after breaking off. Skink females stay with their eggs and remain with the young for a few days after they hatch to keep them safe.

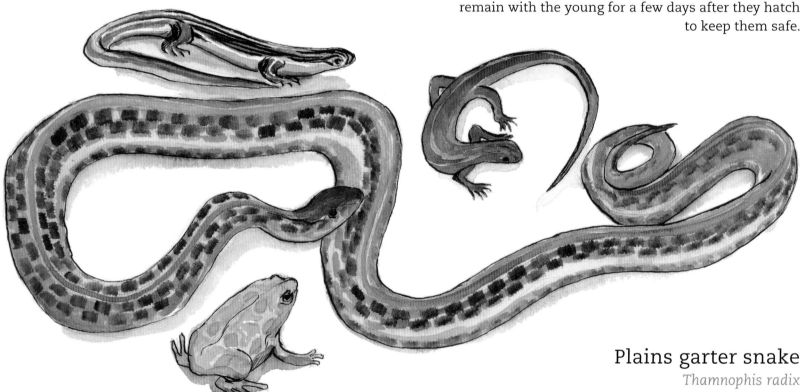

Plains garter snake

Thamnophis radix

Plains garter snakes give off a really strong smell if they are frightened. These snakes hibernate in burrows or holes with other snakes during the winter.

Great Plains toad

Anaxyrus cognatus

Prairies are often dry places, so toads that live there lay their eggs in shallow, temporary ponds. In hot, dry weather, the toads burrow underground to wait for rain.

Insects

Bumblebee *Bombus sp.*

Many kinds of bees, including carpenter bees, miner bees, leaf cutter bees, and mason bees, carry pollen from flower to flower as they gather nectar for food. On a sunny summer day an entire prairie can hum with bees.

Dakota skipper *Hesperia dacotae*

These small butterflies survive only on native prairie (prairie that has never been completely plowed under or destroyed). Dakota skippers are found in North Dakota, South Dakota, and Minnesota, where they are listed as threatened.

Great spangled fritillary *Speyeria cybele*

These beautiful orange and brown butterflies can have up to a four-inch wingspan. Adult butterflies feed on many prairie flowers, including milkweed, bergamot, black-eyed Susan, and Joe Pye weed.

Monarch butterfly *Danaus plexippus*

Monarchs migrate thousands of miles to lay their eggs on milkweed plants. The larvae eat the milkweed leaves, while adults feed on many kinds of flowers, including goldenrods, sunflowers, and asters.

Ottoe skipper butterfly *Hesperia ottoe*

These small brown butterflies survive only in native prairie that has not been plowed or overgrazed. The larvae make tiny shelters of plant material and silk and emerge only to feed on grasses. They are listed as threatened in Minnesota.

Silvery checkerspot butterfly *Chlosyne nycteis*

These small butterflies spend their first winter after the eggs hatch as larvae before making their chrysalises and emerging as adults. Adults eat nectar from prairie plants such as milkweed and fleabane.

Soldier beetle *Chauliognathus pensylvanicus*

Often seen on goldenrod in late summer and fall, these brightly colored beetles eat nectar and many small insects. They look like lightless fireflies.

Red-legged grasshopper *Melanoplus femurrubrum*

Red-legged grasshoppers can fly close to the ground for thirty or forty feet. During a drought, when food is scarce, adults can develop longer wings and fly more often and for longer distances in search of food.

Tiger swallowtail *Papilio glaucus*

These large yellow butterflies feed on golden Alexanders and other flowers. They sometimes "puddle" in large groups, sipping moisture from damp ground.

Flowers

Rough blazing star *Liatris aspera*

Many varieties of blazing star dot the prairie with their blooms in late summer and fall—rough blazing star, dotted blazing star, scaly blazing star, and prairie blazing star. They provide food for butterflies, especially for monarchs as they migrate.

Bottle gentian *Gentiana andrewsii*

Bottle gentian is also called closed gentian because its flowers stay tightly shut. Bumblebees work hard to get at the pollen inside, using their hind legs to hold the petals open so they can get out again.

Butterfly weed *Asclepias tuberosa*

The leaves of this bright orange-blossomed plant are food for monarch butterfly larvae and for gray hairstreak butterfly larvae. Hummingbirds, swallowtails, and other butterflies eat the flowers' nectar.

Cup plant *Silphium perfoliatum*

The leaves of this plant join together at the stem, forming little cups in which rainwater collects. Birds drink this water, and tree frogs sometimes sit in the tiny pools. In the fall, goldfinches dine on the seeds.

Silky aster *Symphyotrichum sericeum*

Many kinds of asters grow in prairies—aromatic asters, New England asters, heath asters, smooth blue asters, and swamp asters. Silky asters have purple-blue flowers.

Foxglove beardtongue *Penstemon digitalis*

Bees and hummingbirds visit this tall flower with tube-shaped blossoms. It blooms in the spring.

Goldenrod *Solidago rigida*

Several kinds of goldenrods bloom in the prairie through late summer and early fall, glowing in the sunshine and providing food for butterflies, beetles, and other insects.

Hairy mountain mint

Pycnanthemum verticillatum variety *pilosum*

You will know if you are walking on mint because its scent will fill the air. Plants that belong to the mint family have a square stem.

Joe Pye weed *Eupatorium maculatum*

Butterflies love the flowers of this tall purplish-pink plant that grows in the wet areas of prairies.

Pale purple coneflower *Echinacea angustifolia*

Goldfinches eat coneflower seeds and butterflies sip nectar from pale purple coneflowers just as they do from grey-headed coneflowers, another prairie flower.

Prairie milkweed *Asclepias sullivantii*

Many kinds of milkweed (common, showy) grow in prairies, offering nectar for insects and butterflies and food for monarch butterfly larvae. On a warm, humid day the scent from a patch of milkweed fills the air. In Minnesota, the common name for *Asclepias sullivantii* is Sullivant's milkweed.

Prairie sunflower *Helianthus petiolaris*

These plants can grow so closely together that they look like a small bush. Their seeds are food for many kinds of birds.

Grasses

Big bluestem   *Andropogon gerardii*

This is a common prairie grass. In summer this tall grass is greenish blue, and in fall it turns purplish red. Big bluestem is often called turkey foot because the stems of its seed heads look like a turkey's footprint.

Indian grass
Sorghastrum nutans

Like bluestem, this grass is found in many kinds of prairies, and its seeds are food for finches and sparrows during the winter.

Prairie plants, left to right: hairy mountain mint, rough blazing star, butterfly weed, pale purple coneflower, prairie milkweed, prairie sunflower, foxglove beardtongue, Indian grass, goldenrod, big bluestem, Joe Pye weed, silky aster, cup plant, bottle gentian.

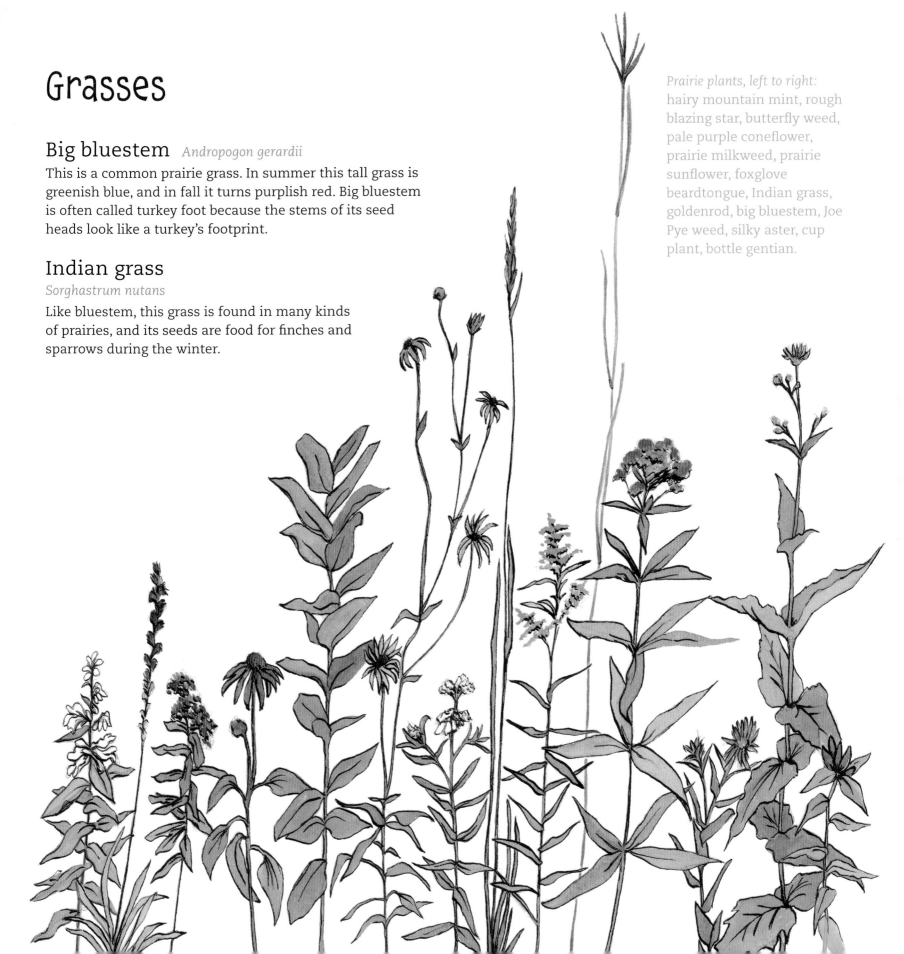

How Gone Is Gone?

Many plants and animals of the prairies have become extinct or extirpated. An extinct animal or plant has disappeared completely from all the places it used to live. If a plant or animal is extirpated, it has vanished from a place where it used to be but might still be found in other places.

Naturalists use three categories to classify native plants and animals that might be in trouble of losing habitat or disappearing altogether.

Endangered: An endangered species is any native plant or animal in danger of disappearing throughout all or most of its range.

Threatened: A threatened species is likely to become endangered in the future because of habitat loss or shrinking numbers.

Of special concern: A plant or animal of special concern is either very rare or has very specific needs for habitat and could become threatened or even endangered.

Where to Find Prairie

Even though less than one-tenth of one percent of native prairie remains in Minnesota, you can still visit patches of prairie, some tiny and some bigger. Here are places where you can see prairie plants and animals.

State Parks

Pieces of prairie have been preserved or restored in many state parks, including Blue Mounds State Park, Buffalo River State Park, Kilen Woods State Park, Big Stone Lake State Park, and Glacial Lakes State Park. Learn more about prairies in Minnesota state parks in *Prairie, Lake, Forest: Minnesota's State Parks* and also at www.dnr.state.mn.us.

Scientific and Natural Areas

Many scientific and natural areas in Minnesota preserve remnants of prairie. Bluestem Prairie, Des Moines River, and Prairie Smoke Dunes are scientific and natural areas with larger prairie remnants. Small but rich remnants grow at Iron Horse Prairie, Butternut Valley Prairie, and Joseph A. Tauer Prairie. You can find out more in *A Guide to Minnesota's Scientific and Natural Areas* and also at www.dnr.state.mn.us.

Nature Conservancy Preserves

The Nature Conservancy has protected many prairie areas, including Pembina Trail Preserve, Ordway Prairie, Regal Meadow Preserve, Schaefer Prairie, and Hole in the Mountain Prairie. You can learn more about these prairies in *Prairies, Woods, and Islands: A Guide to the Minnesota Preserves of the Nature Conservancy* and at www.nature.org.

Find a Pocket of Prairie

Tiny pockets of prairie exist in places where you don't expect them: in ditches along roadsides that haven't been sprayed, in former railroad rights of way, in old cemeteries. An unplowed field may still contain the seeds of prairie plants that sprout up when they have the chance. If you look carefully, you may discover your own pockets of prairie.

We can't bring back the great prairie or the herds of bison, but we can cherish the prairie that is left and plant our own little pockets of prairie, hoping that prairie insects, birds, and other animals might come to these plants and find a home.

Phyllis Root loves to visit prairie wherever she can find it—a few acres or hundreds of acres—at a park or a preserve or an old cemetery. Once she and a friend found a rare western prairie fringed orchid where no one had seen one for thirty years (then they lost it and had to find it all over again). Her yard is full of prairie plants, and she is never happier than when she is looking at native flowers under a prairie sky.

Betsy Bowen lives in the north woods and is refreshed by the contrast of the open space of the prairies. So much sky! She likes to stare up at it and let her mind wander.